LEADERSHIP in 5G

COMPANION WORKBOOK

50 EXERCISES TO UPGRADE YOUR LEADERSHIP

HOWARD C. FERO, PHD

Copyright © 2025 by Howard Fero, all rights reserved.

No part of this publication may be reproduced, distributed, or transmitted in any form or by any means, including photocopying, recording, or other electronic or mechanical methods without the prior written permission of the publisher, except in the case of brief quotations embodied in critical reviews and certain other noncommercial uses permitted by copyright law. For permission requests write to the publisher, address "Attention Permissions Coordinator," at the address below.

The Leadership Doc, LLC
PO Box 110773
Trumbull, CT 06611
www.theleadershipdoc.com
203-983-0983
ISBN: 978-0-9960880-4-6

Table of Contents

LEADERSHIP IN 5G COMPANION WORKBOOK 1

THE 5GS OF LEADERSHIP 3

GET UP 5
    1. We are All Leaders 6
    2. Leaders Are Humble 8
    3. Leaders Are Purpose-Driven 9
    4. Leaders Are Passion-Driven 10
    5. Leaders Are Mission-Driven 12
    6. Leaders Are Self-Aware 13
    7. Leaders Are Mindful 15
    8. S.M.A.R.T. Goals 17
    9. The Modified Open-Door Policy 19
    10. Accountability 20
    11. Time Management 22
    12. Urgent vs Important 23

GET OUT THERE 25
    13. The TALK Model of Communication 26
    14. Be Optimistic but Realistic 28
    15. When Possible – Be Positive! 29
    16. Keep It Specific 30
    17. Presence Is Everything 32
    18. Know Your Communication Style 33
    19. Share Your Decision-Making Strategies 35
    20. Delivering Bad News 36
    21. Leading By Example 38
    22. Your Personal Board of Directors 39
    23. Leaders Don't Have All the Answers 40

GET TO KNOW YOUR PEOPLE 43
    24. The Power of the Follower 44
    25. Building Trust 45
    26. The "Platinum Rule" 46
    27. Making Yourself Available – How Can I Help? 48
    28. When You Ask for Feedback – Listen 49
    29. Prioritize One-on-One's 50
    30. Create Memories that Matter 51

GIVE THEM WHAT THEY NEED..53
   31. A New Generation of Needs...54
   32. Psychological Safety and Building Confidence.........................56
   33. Help Others See the Mission and Vision..................................57
   34. Trust and Respect..58
   35. The Right Seat on the Bus..60
   36. Training..62
   37. Mentorship...63
   38. Feedback..64
   39. Helping Others Build the Life They Want................................65
   40. Rejuvenation..67
   41. Leading in Uncertain Times...69

GET OUT OF THE WAY!..71
   42. A Well-Oiled Machine...72
   43. Decision-Making...73
   44. Situational Leadership..74
   45. Leading People Toward the "Win"...75
   46. A Continual Focus on the "Next Thing".................................77
   47. The Link Between Winning and Purpose................................80
   48. Learning From Mistakes...81
   49. When We Are Proactive, We Don't Need to Be Reactive..........82
   50. Leaving a Legacy..83

ACTION ITEMS...87

Leadership in 5G Companion Workbook

When Leadership in 5G was published, I hoped its principles would encourage leaders everywhere to conceptualize leadership in a new way: a way that can transform both your personal and professional lives. The response from readers, students, and clients has been encouraging, and when I work with clients, I hear and see the many ways that they are encouraging their leaders to Get Up, Get Out There, Get to Know Their People, Give Them What They Need, and Get Out of the Way!

The incredible feedback I've received, along with the work I've done alongside clients and students, are the foundation of this workbook. Changing your thinking is one part of the battle; changing your actions is the next (and arguably more important) part!

As you work through the Leadership in 5G Companion Workbook, it's my hope that you will refer back to *Leadership in 5G* to review the concepts in more depth. Even more so, it's my hope that you will utilize the last pages of the book as you work through the exercises to identify your next steps and action items. How you take the work that you've done and apply it to practice is the key to success. Much effort has gone into creating these exercises, and they have proven quite useful with those who have worked through them.

The Companion Workbook is organized similar to *Leadership in 5G*, structured around the 5Gs of Leadership and providing opportunities for you to apply them to practice. The workbook is meant to be used in conjunction with the book, as it's in the book where you will find the concepts explored in more depth and with illustrative examples.

Before you begin your work here, I'll ask you to turn to Page 87, where you'll find pages for you to identify specific Action Items. Throughout the book, you'll find exercises to get you thinking (and doing!), and for many of them, I will prompt you to add an item to your Action Item list in the back. My last piece of advice, and my last 'ask' here, is don't wait for my prompts! As you think of something to do to enhance your leadership, head to the back, write a specific action item, and **Get to Work**!

The 5Gs of Leadership

Get Up. This G is about *you*. How well do you really know yourself? Do you know your leadership style? Have you mastered self-management? Discovering your purpose and the things you are passionate about are critical to knowing who you are as a leader. Executing effectively as a leader means knowing how to set goals and achieve them, manage your time, and lead yourself.

Get Out There. This G is about how you show up amongst the people you lead. How do you build trust? How do you communicate? Who needs to know what, when, and why? It involves strategically involving other people in your personal growth journey and being a leader who is both seen and heard, not leading from afar.

Get to Know Your People. Getting to know your people is just how it sounds; it's about understanding who is on your team and what makes them tick. People love to be known, and when they feel that way, they naturally want to work harder. When you know your people, you can provide effective feedback in the best received style. An organizational culture where people are known is one where they can thrive.

Give Them What They Need. Once you know your people, you better know how to equip them for success. A person's needs transcend their job training; each person has varying priorities, personalities, goals, and strengths and weaknesses. Building an environment and a role tailored to each person's unique needs profoundly impacts retention and employee satisfaction.

Get Out of the Way! Many leaders love to be involved in the details but choose the wrong ones to involve themselves with. If you've hired the right people, gotten to know them, and given them what they need, the organization should be equipped to run like a well-oiled machine. This frees you up to focus on the bigger-picture aspects of mission, vision, and long-term success.

GET UP

Being a self-leader is to serve as chief, captain, president, or CEO of one's own life
PETER DRUCKER

Before we can lead others effectively, we must first lead ourselves. We need to understand our why and our how, considering best practices so that we can be 'our best self.' When people encounter the material in our first 'G,' "Get Up," the most common reaction is 'aha.' They realize that they know a bit about their strengths and understand some of the areas they need to develop, but they also acknowledge that they haven't put much thought into leveraging their strengths on a consistent basis. To be successful leaders, we need to Get Up, figuratively and literally, and learn about ourselves, our passions, our purpose, our strengths, our weaknesses, our tendencies, and more. We need to do a deep dive within so we can become our strongest selves.

The exercises in Get Up are designed to help you look within yourself and develop a better concept of who you are as a leader.

1. We are All Leaders

> *The most dangerous leadership myth is that leaders are born, that there is a genetic factor to leadership. This myth asserts that people simply either have certain charismatic qualities or not. That's nonsense; in fact, the opposite is true. Leaders are made rather than born.*
> — Warren Bennis

Quite often, we find ourselves in leadership positions, either formally or informally. Sometimes, we aspire to them, and sometimes, we simply find ourselves there. No matter how or why we find ourselves leading, we need to remember that we have many leadership strengths; the key is to leverage them and continue to develop them to make them even stronger. We can always become a better leader, and awareness of who we are is the first step.

Exercise 1: My Leadership Abilities

Instructions: For each leadership attribute below, rank yourself on a scale from 1 to 5 by circling the number that best represents your current abilities. Be honest in your assessment as you identify your strengths and areas for growth.

Scale: 1 - Limited | 2 - Emerging | 3 - Moderate | 4 - Strong | 5 - Exceptional Strength

Self-Awareness 1 2 3 4 5	Integrity 1 2 3 4 5	Coaching & Mentoring 1 2 3 4 5
Accountability 1 2 3 4 5	Confidence 1 2 3 4 5	Influence 1 2 3 4 5
Decision-Making 1 2 3 4 5	Resilience 1 2 3 4 5	Emotional Intelligence 1 2 3 4 5
Communication 1 2 3 4 5	Vision 1 2 3 4 5	Problem-Solving 1 2 3 4 5
Adaptability 1 2 3 4 5	Strategic Thinking 1 2 3 4 5	Initiative 1 2 3 4 5
Team Collaboration 1 2 3 4 5	Empathy 1 2 3 4 5	Time Management 1 2 3 4 5
Delegation 1 2 3 4 5	Creativity 1 2 3 4 5	Relationship-Building 1 2 3 4 5
Conflict Resolution 1 2 3 4 5	Open-Mindedness 1 2 3 4 5	Innovation 1 2 3 4 5
Courage 1 2 3 4 5	Persuasion 1 2 3 4 5	Growth Mindset 1 2 3 4 5
Cultural Awareness 1 2 3 4 5	Negotiation 1 2 3 4 5	Active Listening 1 2 3 4 5
Collaboration 1 2 3 4 5	Transparency 1 2 3 4 5	Dependability 1 2 3 4 5
Humility 1 2 3 4 5	Risk Management 1 2 3 4 5	Patience 1 2 3 4 5
Servant Leadership 1 2 3 4 5	Motivation 1 2 3 4 5	Crisis Management 1 2 3 4 5
Delegation 1 2 3 4 5	Initiative 1 2 3 4 5	Decision Agility 1 2 3 4 5
Ethical Leadership 1 2 3 4 5	Influence 1 2 3 4 5	Professionalism 1 2 3 4 5

My Three Primary Leadership Strengths:

1. _____

2. _____

3. _____

Three Areas I Want To Improve:

1. _____

2. _____

3. _____

Three Ways I Can Develop My Skills (ex., books, training programs, mentors, etc.). Be specific!

1. _____

2. _____

3. _____

2. Leaders Are Humble

> *A leader is best when people barely know he exists; when his work is done, his aim fulfilled, they will say: we did it ourselves.*
> — Lao Tzu

Humility is a core tenet of leadership. It's not about seeking personal gain or recognition but about helping others reach a shared goal. A humble leader puts the team's needs first, guiding them with integrity and care, and in doing so, earns respect and fosters a culture of collaboration and trust. True leadership is about empowering others, not elevating oneself.

Exercise 2: Conquering Ego

Has there been a time when your ego got in the way of your leadership? What do you wish you had done differently to behave like a more humble leader?

Example:

Ego-driven: I lost my cool in a meeting because I felt personally attacked by someone's feedback.

Humble: I shouldn't allow my identity or sense of security to be challenged by another person. Keeping control of my emotions is my job, and it's more productive to focus on the task at hand rather than defending myself.

I let my ego get in the way when…

_____

_____

_____

To act as a more humble leader, I could have…

_____

_____

_____

Example:

We might have found an actual solution to the problem at hand if I had not been distracted by my own anger or sense of being threatened.

If I reacted differently, the outcome could have looked more like this…

_____

_____

_____

_____

3. Leaders Are Purpose-Driven

> *There is no failure except failure to serve one's purpose.*
> — HENRY FORD

When we care about something that goes beyond our personal success, we work harder. This is a core of purpose-driven leadership. Think back to Mark Twain's quote from **Leadership in 5G**, "The two most important days in your life are the day you are born and the day you find out why."

Exercise 3: Becoming Purpose-Driven

Create a purpose statement for your life. What is your purpose? Think about the things that are important to you, and then think about what you are doing each day to contribute to that cause.

Examples:

- *My purpose is to utilize my natural skills and abilities to make the world around me a better place.*
- *My purpose is to use my creativity to build products that change the world.*
- *My purpose is to develop confidence in others around me.*

My purpose is to…

_____

_____

_____

_____

What are three ways you can turn your purpose statement into action? These actions can be small steps. Think of ways you can apply your purpose in your workplace, by volunteering, or through other opportunities.

1. _____

2. _____

3. _____

4. Leaders Are Passion-Driven

> *A mediocre idea that generates enthusiasm will go further than a great idea that inspires no one.*
> — MARY KAY ASH

Flow is a theory of motivation that focuses on our ability to enter a state of peak experience in which we are fully engaged in what we are doing without a necessary focus on the outcome. When we achieve Flow, we're finding satisfaction from the process itself and, with that, performing at our optimal level. We often find that we lose our sense of time when we're in a Flow state, as we're so immersed in the activity that we feel we could do it endlessly. This state is often achieved when we're performing activities that tap into our sense of passion. It comes when we are challenged and when we have the skills we need to overcome the challenge.

Exercise 4: Flow

Think about times in your work when you felt completely absorbed, focused, and motivated. These could be times when you lost track of time, felt a sense of effortless achievement, or experienced deep satisfaction in what you were doing.

In the table below, write down 3-5 specific activities or tasks where you have experienced flow. For each one, reflect on the activity you were doing and the factors that contributed to you entering a flow state (e.g., the challenge of the task, your level of skill, your interest in the subject matter), along with the emotions involved. (How did you feel during and after the experience?)

ACTIVITY/TASK	FACTORS CONTRIBUTING TO FLOW	EMOTIONS DURING THE EXPERIENCE	EMOTIONS AFTER THE EXPERIENCE

Are there tasks or activities at work that you enjoy or excel at but aren't currently doing regularly? What can you do to incorporate these tasks more often into your routine? Identify three specific actions you can take to create opportunities for Flow at work.

1. _____

2. _____

3. _____

5. Leaders Are Mission-Driven

> *Efforts and courage are not enough without purpose and direction.*
> — John F. Kennedy

Every organization has a mission, a vision, a strategy, and a focus that drives what they're trying to achieve. Your organization's mission should clearly state who you serve and in what way you intend to serve them. The mission should guide you, inspire you, and empower you to help move the organization forward. In order for the mission to have this impact on you, you need to know how what you do each day will help to further it.

Exercise 5: Leaning into Mission

My Organization's Mission Statement:

_____

_____

_____

_____

_____

How do you and your role fit into the mission? What are some ways your role in the organization works to further it?

Example:

Mission statement: Our mission is to preserve the natural environment through education, advocacy, and direct action.

My role: As a human resources leader, I can advance this mission by ensuring that our new recruits feel passionate about this mission and are consistently well-educated in how to bring this mission to life.

Specific ways that my daily actions contribute to advancing my organization's mission:

1. _____

2. _____

3. _____

Identify three ways that you can do more to help further the organization's mission.

Example:

I can set aside one afternoon this month to examine what training opportunities exist for my staff. I will start by asking the staff what opportunities they are interested in.

1. _____

2. _____

3. _____

What impact will these enhancements have on those you work with and/or the customers you serve?

_____

_____

_____

_____

CREATE AN ACTION ITEM — GO TO PAGE 87

6. Leaders Are Self-Aware

There are three things (that are) extremely hard: steel, a diamond, and to know one's self.
— Benjamin Franklin

One of my favorite workshops to facilitate explores the four leadership archetypes below. We spend time understanding them and then, through various activities, determine how to work best with people who are similar and different from ourselves. It's fun and eye-opening, and participants leave with practical tools and direction. The four archetypes are: the Go-Getter, the Researcher, the Empath, and the Visionary.

The Go-Getter: This type of leader is going to go out there and push, push, push. They are the ones who like to be in front, leading the way.

The Researcher: This type of leader likes to do all their homework before they make any decisions. They want all their T's crossed and their I's dotted, making sure everything is lined up perfectly before they move forward.

The Empath: Before this type of leader does anything, they want to think about how their actions are going to impact their team, the rest of their organization, and anybody involved.

The Visionary: The fourth type of leader is the big-picture visionary thinker. This person is innovative and creative and has lots of ideas. This leader isn't as focused on the details, which can sometimes lead to issues!

Exercise 6: The Leader Archetype

Consider your own style of leadership. When you think about these four archetypes, reflect on what your natural tendencies are. Which archetype describes you best?

Example:

I see myself as a visionary. I get the most energized when I'm ideating and dreaming of how things could be different. I get exasperated or bogged down by details.

My strongest archetype: _____

Some of the benefits of having this style:

1. _____

2. _____

3. _____

Some of the challenges of working with this style:

1. _____

2. _____

3. _____

The most successful teams are composed of varying archetypes. Our leadership benefits a situation most when we work alongside people with a different archetype than we are, as it is important that each dimension is represented. Consider a team you are currently a part of. Are each of the archetypes represented?

Identify an area where your team is strong and one which is lacking. Consider ways to enhance your team with a focus on each of the dimensions.

Example:

Our leadership team is missing someone with the gift of empathy. We have great ideas, a strong drive, and attention to detail, but we sometimes miss the impact our decisions have on the real lives of our employees. Brandon, our VP of Marketing, seems better attuned to the needs of people. When we're implementing widespread organizational changes, we could invite him into these conversations to ensure we're thinking of everyone's needs and employee morale more than just the bottom line.

A team I am currently on is comprised of people with the following archetypes (if you aren't currently on a team, consider one you have been on in the past):

_____

_____

_____

_____

One of the missing archetypes is the _____. It would be beneficial to call on _____ (identify someone in your organization) for their perspective on a future project.

CREATE AN ACTION ITEM
GO TO PAGE 87

7. Leaders Are Mindful

Mindfulness improves your capacity for self-discovery and empowerment.
— Amit Ray

You need to be in a good place emotionally and personally to be able to give and do for others. When you're balanced in these areas, you're better able to connect with yourself and others, making mindfulness practices more meaningful and effective.

Exercise 7: Mindfulness

What helps you feel refreshed? Make a list of activities that help clear your mind so you can be a more focused and stronger leader.

1. _____

2. _____

3. _____

4. _____

5. _____

Think of a time when you tried to lead but weren't functioning at your best? What might have been different if you were at full capacity?

_____

_____

_____

_____

Identify three mindfulness activities you can take prior to a meeting or work task to optimize your focus.

1. _____

2. _____

3. _____

8. S.M.A.R.T. Goals

One part at a time, one day at a time, we can accomplish any goal we set for ourselves.
— Karen Casey

Whether you're setting individual or team goals, remember that all goals should be S.M.A.R.T.: Specific, Measurable, Action-Oriented, Realistic, and Time and Resource-Constrained.

Exercise 8: S.M.A.R.T. Goals

Write a S.M.A.R.T. goal. What do you wish to achieve in the near future?

Examples:

- *Improve team productivity by 15 percent within the next six months by implementing an innovative project management tool.*
- *In the next six months, I will develop my management skills through mentorship, with at least two mentees from either our company's Employee Resource Groups or my alumni network. I will identify my mentees within two weeks, reach out to them in the following week with my intent, and schedule a meeting with them at the beginning of the following month. We will meet monthly and have action items and discussion points ready for each session.*

My S.M.A.R.T. Goal

_____

_____

_____

_____

What makes it S.M.A.R.T?

Specific:

_____

_____

_____

Measurable:
_____
_____
_____
_____

Action-Oriented:
_____
_____
_____
_____

Realistic:
_____
_____
_____
_____

Time and Resource Constrained:
_____
_____
_____
_____

Bonus: Refer back to Exercise 1. Using the S.M.A.R.T. framework, create a goal to enhance one of the leadership abilities you identified as an area to improve.

_____

_____

_____

_____

9. The Modified Open-Door Policy

A leader is one who knows the way, goes the way, and shows the way.
— JOHN C. MAXWELL

We all love the idea of an open-door policy; in theory, it's great, as we should always be there for our people. The reality, however, is that a true open-door policy isn't always possible as we have plenty of individual work that we need to get done. Being interrupted is not conducive to being efficient and effective. A modified open-door policy lets our people know that we are there for them 24/7 for emergencies, BUT, if something *can* wait until our 'open time,' we'd appreciate it. What's most important about a modified open-door policy is that it's communicated clearly and respectfully to our teams. Before we can communicate it to our teams, we need to first be clear with our structure.

Exercise 9: The Modified Open-Door Policy

Design your personal "modified open-door policy" by creating a weekly schedule that includes specific blocks of time for personal work and designated availability for your team.

Example:

Mondays, Wednesdays, and Fridays from 10-2, I will hang a sign on my door that says, "I'm engaged in focused work. Please wait if you can!"

_____

_____

_____

_____

Take it further: Share your plan with your team and explain to them how it benefits both their needs and your productivity. Encourage them to create blocks of focused work time for themselves that are uninterrupted by questions or meetings, and help them communicate this to the rest of the team clearly and kindly.

10. Accountability

> *Be faithful in small things because it is in them that your strength lies.*
> — MOTHER TERESA

One of the primary ways we build trust with our team is by following through with our promises. If we promise a team member that we will be considering (or addressing) an issue, we need to make sure that we are doing so! This is the foundation of relationships, albeit personal or professional. To be an effective leader, we need to be accountable to ourselves as well as those with whom we work.

Exercise 10: A Test of Follow-Through

When was the last time you didn't follow through on your word? What was the impact?

Example: I told an employee we would do her performance review by the end of the week. This was two weeks ago, and I can sense her growing cold. I know performance reviews are incredibly important to people, and it can be stressful when they are waiting. I allowed this to happen because I wasn't intentional with my time management, but that is not an excuse.

_____

_____

_____

_____

What are three things you've promised others lately but have yet to follow through on?

Examples:

- *I told my daughter I'd take her out for ice cream.*
- *I told my wife I would clean the gutters.*
- *I told my employee I would respond to the email they sent with new ideas for the team.*

1. _____

2. _____

3. _____

What are three work-related promises you've made to others **and did** follow through on?

1. _____

2. _____

3. _____

What impact did the follow-through and/or lack of follow-through have on your relationships?

11. Time Management

I must govern the clock, not be governed by it.
— GOLDA MEIR

Scheduling is a non-negotiable priority! It's important to schedule time to relax, work on projects, make phone calls, etc., anything we know we won't do automatically. Many of us say we'll do 'our work' in between meetings, not putting this on our calendar, just 'fitting it in.' This lessens the importance of those tasks and makes them harder to accomplish. Use your calendar wisely. Enter your tasks in the time you have available. Accomplishing what we have listed on our calendar is quite rewarding, so the more we can 'check items off our list,' the more motivated we will be. Set yourself up for success, use your time wisely, and, in turn, you'll be in a better position to lead yourself and others more effectively.

Exercise 11: Using the Calendar to Our Advantage

How can you use your schedule more effectively to better accomplish your tasks? Look at your calendar and the time you have 'in between' your meetings this week.

List three tasks that you need to accomplish, along with how much time it will take to accomplish them.

1. _____

2. _____

3. _____

Find open time on your calendar and enter these tasks into those slots. Use this opportunity to enter time on your calendar for reflection and development as well. Reading, meditating, or simply taking a walk are often done 'when we have time' as opposed to being scheduled, and 'when we have time' doesn't often happen if we don't schedule it!

Head to the Action Items pages at the end of this book and write, "Schedule work and home tasks, along with time to relax and recharge, on the calendar each week."

Put a check here when you've done it! ____

12. Urgent vs Important

> *There are important and urgent matters, but what is important is not always urgent and what is urgent is not always important. It's a leader's responsibility to know and understand the difference.*
> — DWIGHT EISENHOWER

As a leader, it's important to recognize the difference between tasks that are urgent and those that are truly important. Urgent tasks demand your immediate attention, but important tasks are the ones that drive real progress. If you spend all your time putting out fires, you might miss opportunities to lead effectively.

Exercise 12: Urgent vs Important

Take a moment to reflect on your week. List three tasks you completed:

1. _____

2. _____

3. _____

Now, consider each one: Was it urgent, important, or both? Are you spending your time where it matters most? What adjustments can you make to better prioritize your leadership?

_____

_____

_____

_____

GET OUT THERE

The art of communication is the language of leadership.
- James C. Humes

The second "G," Get Up, is all about communication, visibility, and collaboration. No matter how much you grow personally, if others can't see or hear those changes, your leadership won't have the impact it should. Leadership doesn't happen in a vacuum; people need to see your actions, hear your support, and feel your guidance. While communication might come more naturally to some, it's an essential part of being an effective leader.

The focus of *Get Out There* is on using communication and presence to lead effectively. Leaders need to actively engage with their teams, not just be self-aware, they incorporate the TALK Mode and focus on positive communication whenever possible. 5G Leaders lead by example, creating an environment of confidence and collaboration.

The exercises in *Get Out There* are designed to help you develop the critical skills of communication, visibility, and collaboration that are essential for effective leadership

13. The TALK Model of Communication

Communication is a skill that you can learn. It's like riding a bicycle or typing. If you're willing to work at it, you can rapidly improve the quality of every part of your life."
— BRIAN TRACY

The TALK model of communication is something I developed to help leaders remember a few basic principles to guide their communication. This is a model of communication that puts relationships first and gives people a chance to listen because they want to, not because they have to.

> **TALK Model:**
>
> **T**ell them the truth.
> **A**cknowledge their ideas.
> **L**oyalty is key.
> **K**now your people.

Exercise 13: Let's TALK

Think about something you'd like to communicate to a colleague or to your team. In a sentence or two, what is the message?

_____

_____

_____

_____

Tell them the truth. Are there aspects of what you would like to communicate that you hesitate to share? Could your message be more transparent? Would the message benefit from more details and a focus on why it is important? Share some ideas here as to how you can expand on the message, including more details about its importance and impact.

_____

_____

_____

_____

Acknowledge their ideas. Think about a message you have communicated to your team in the past. Did you consider everyone's potential contribution to this topic? Is there anyone you might have missed? How much effort did you put into making sure people not only had the chance to share but also ample time to think about their ideas? Identify three ways that you could have given more attention to one or more of your team members. What are some ways this could have impacted the outcome?

_____

_____

_____

_____

Loyalty is key. Based on the current or past message you have been considering, is there anything you could say to your team that reminds them that you're there to support them? What are some ways that you can communicate this to them?

_____

_____

_____

_____

Know your people. How does your information need to be tailored to the different people on your team? Have you considered how it will impact people in different roles? What about different work styles? Have you provided data for the data-oriented people and covered how it will impact human beings for the empathy minded people? Identify specific ways your team's differences could/should have impacted the message.

_____

_____

_____

_____

14. Be Optimistic but Realistic

> *Optimism isn't a belief that things will automatically get better;*
> *it's a conviction that we can make things better.*
> — MELINDA GATES

When rolling out a new initiative, how you communicate has a major impact on how your team responds. It's important to be upfront about challenges, but focusing too much on the negatives can create resistance. Finding a balance between being realistic and optimistic helps your team stay confident while also preparing them for what's coming. This exercise will help you craft messages that motivate your team and keep them engaged, even when facing challenges.

Exercise 14: Introducing a New Initiative

Take some time to reflect: Do you think you tend to lean toward the positive or the negative when sharing information with your team? Consider a message you have given to your team; can you adjust it to have a more positive (but still realistic) spin? Share your message below.

Example: We are going to be introducing a new sales management tool. The tool will help you tremendously in tracking your prospects, but I admit there is a bit of a learning curve. I'm confident you are going to find it useful, but wait a few weeks before you pass judgment. For the next several weeks, you probably won't be feeling as positive about the change!

Do you lean toward the positive or negative when sharing information with your team?

_____

_____

_____

Consider a message you've shared with your team recently. What was the overall tone?

_____

_____

_____

Now, adjust that message to make it more positive while still being realistic.

What are some ways this change of focus/delivery may have impacted the next steps?

15. When Possible – Be Positive!

> *Positive leadership is often interpreted as touchy-feely. But the evidence over the last 10 years is clear: if you implement it, performance and customer satisfaction go up. The duty of a leader is to create an organization where it is easy to practice kindness.*
> — CAMERON

Kim Cameron's research revealed that high-performing teams received 5.6 positive comments for every negative comment that was expressed.

If you have a positive outlook and communicate with more positive messages, your organization will produce greater results. It's that simple.

Exercise 15: Focusing on the Positive

Spend a week tracking yourself. Set up a "note" on your phone with a place to identify the positive and negative things you say at work (you can try this at home, too; those you live with will appreciate it!). Notate each time you say something positive and each time you say something negative during the week. Come back here and write your ratio (if you're a math person, go ahead and simplify it to see how it compares to the nearly 6:1 ratio Cameron identified). Most likely, you will have some work to do. Make a pledge to include more positivity in your communication.

Week of _____ to _____

Number of Positive Messages __ Number of Negative Messages __ My Ration __:__

What I learned...

_____

_____

_____

_____

16. Keep It Specific

If you just communicate, you can get by. But if you communicate skillfully, you can work miracles.
— Jim Rohn

When a team member is not confident in the message that we delivered, it can cause great anxiety. Though we may hope that person follows up with any clarifying questions they may have, the most efficient way to address this potential anxiety is to avoid it in the first place! As many scholars have said, 'clarity is brevity'!

Exercise 16: Keep It Simple!

Look back at three recent emails you sent and consider how they could have been more specific. Put yourself in the other person's shoes, assuming they might have some level of anxiety about doing a job well or worrying about asking you unnecessary questions.

Example: In my last email to my assistant, I instructed him to make sure the report was "comprehensive." I can see how that request was vague and could have resulted in his anxiety, assuming that he should 'know' what being comprehensive means. I remember in the past when he spent several hours doing the wrong task because he interpreted something like that differently than I intended it. Next time, I could specify that I wanted the datasets linked to each section of the report.

Review a recent email you sent. What was unclear or vague in your message?

_____

_____

_____

_____

How might the recipient have felt or reacted to that lack of clarity?

_____

_____

_____

_____

How would you rewrite the email to be more specific and action focused?

_____

_____

_____

_____

17. Presence Is Everything

> *Clearing your head of distractions in order to notice and understand the people you are with can feel inefficient - there are so many other people and issues to think about. But being present makes you effective.*
> — MARGARET HEFFERNAN

If you've ever been deep in a serious or critical conversation with someone, only to have them pull out their cell phone and start scrolling while saying, "Keep going. I'm listening," you understand how valuable being fully present and focused can be. Being present for those around us is vital for a relationship to thrive. Whether we are in the office, interacting with colleagues, or at home on the couch with our family, when we are *there*, we need to be *there*!

Exercise 17: Present Yourself Fully!

Think of a recent conversation where you felt distracted or disengaged. Why were you distracted?

_____

_____

_____

How did your distractions impact the quality of the conversation or your ability to connect with the other person?

_____

_____

_____

What specific actions can you take during future conversations to be more present?

_____

_____

_____

_____

Bonus Challenge: During work hours, ensure your phone is turned off, turned over, or put away in your desk drawer whenever a colleague or client approaches you.

Doing this demonstrates your attention to the person in front of you and makes them feel valued, helping to foster a stronger relationship.

18. Know Your Communication Style

If one does not understand a person, one tends to regard him as a fool.
— CARL JUNG

Introverts prefer to hear information, take time to think about it, and process it before responding. Extroverts, on the other hand, like to "talk through" their responses; their conversation is how they reason and process their thoughts. If you don't know if your team member is an extrovert or an introvert, you can misread your communications in ways that hurt your relationship. We will always be a better leader when we learn about and understand those around us.

Exercise 18: Communication Styles

How do you prefer to process information? Do you like a quiet space to contemplate, or do you prefer to 'talk through' your ideas?

_____

_____

_____

_____

Identify some ways you can create an environment that will afford you the best opportunity to utilize your preferred style. Does your team know what style you prefer?

_____

_____

_____

_____

As discussed in *Leadership in 5G*, it's important that we know the styles of our people so that we can lead them most effectively. Do you know your team members' preferred style of communication? How can you be more considerate of their communication styles?

_____

_____

_____

_____

Example: In meetings, I can send the agenda ahead of time, including any pieces the team might need input on, so people with internal processing communication styles have time to marinate. I'll check in with them before moving on to a different topic to make sure the extroverts don't talk over them.

_____

_____

_____

_____

19. Share Your Decision-Making Strategies

No one can whistle a symphony. It takes a whole orchestra to play it.
— H.E. Luccock

When formulating a goal, decision, or initiative that will impact our team, it's always more powerful to engage the team in the decision-making process. This approach will lead to increased ownership and commitment from those involved in moving the goal or decision forward. Setting goals as a team leads to better ideas, actions, and outcomes because collaboration has been proven time and time again to be a more effective process than the "lone wolf" approach.

Exercise 19: Collaborative Decision-Making

Describe a decision or initiative you're currently considering. Who will this decision impact? Who should be in the room when the decision is made? In the lines below, share the initiative and your initial plan to move it forward.

_____

_____

_____

_____

Now, add a few more lines that go a bit deeper. Are there additional team members who might have some insight or be able to see the decision from a different angle? How might you incorporate that person or people into the planning and execution stages of the initiative?

___

___

___

___

CREATE AN ACTION ITEM → GO TO PAGE 87

20. Delivering Bad News

> *More information is always better than less. When people know the reason things are happening, even if it's bad news, they can adjust their expectations and react accordingly. Keeping people in the dark only serves to stir negative emotions.*
> — SIMON SINEK

Presenting bad news is often part of our responsibility as a leader. It may be a responsibility we prefer to avoid, but it's a responsibility all the same.

Exercise 20: Making Bad News a Bit Better

Think about the last time you had to deliver bad news. How did it go? Were there any unexpected reactions or challenges?

___

___

___

What was the location and timing of your message? Could either have been improved to make the message easier to digest?

_____

_____

_____

_____

How did your tone come across? Did it help manage the situation or add to the tension?

_____

_____

_____

_____

What three things could you improve the next time you need to deliver bad news? (e.g., location, timing, tone, clarity, offering support, etc.)

1. _____

2. _____

3. _____

CREATE AN ACTION ITEM
GO TO PAGE 87

21. Leading By Example

If you want everyone else to be passionate, committed, dedicated, and motivated, you go first!
— Marshall Goldsmith

Whether we realize it or not, our people are always watching us. They're looking to us for cues on how to act, communicate, and interact. This happens with our employees, team members, friends, and even children. We learn by observation and replicate actions that we deem productive.

Exercise 21: Your Leadership Shadow

If someone followed you around for 48 hours, taking notes on how you treat others, spend your time, and make decisions, what are five things they would observe?

1. _____

2. _____

3. _____

4. _____

5. _____

Now that you've recorded what you think others would observe, what are some ways that you would *prefer* them to see you? Identify three ways you would prefer to be seen:

1. _____

2. _____

3. _____

What specific steps can you take to help you be seen in the manner above?

_____

_____

_____

22. Your Personal Board of Directors

If you cannot see where you are going, ask someone who has been there before.
— J Loren Norris

One of the ways you can keep an eye on your own integrity is through enlisting what I call your "personal board of directors." These are people you can consult when you want to decide how to go about changing your career, growing your career, or helping your team to be more successful. Surrounding ourselves with the right people is one way to make ourselves the strongest we can be.

Exercise 22: Who's Helping Guide You?

Identify three to five people who can offer valuable advice to you if you need it. These can be people from any part of your life, as long as you trust and respect their opinions and that the advice they will give you has your best interest at heart.

1. _____

2. _____

3. _____

4. _____

5. _____

Reach out! Set a timeline for connecting with the people you listed above. Tell them you are putting together your 'personal board of directors' and would like to be able to turn to them with questions once in a while. Go a step further and tell them that you're there for them to serve on their 'board' as well.

Head to the Action Items pages at the end of this book and make a separate item (with a date) that you will reach out to each of your potential 'board members'.

23. Leaders Don't Have All the Answers

Pride is concerned with who is right. Humility is concerned with what is right.
— Ezra Taft Benson

As a leader, you don't need to have all the answers. Your role is to guide your team to find the answers themselves, whether through discussion, reflection, or simply pointing them in the right direction. Accepting that you don't have every solution can be empowering, both for you and your team. It's about fostering the environment that helps others learn and grow.

Exercise 23: How Comfortable Are You With Being Wrong?

Think of a recent time when someone asked you a question and you didn't know the answer. How did you feel at that moment?

_____

_____

_____

How did those feelings (e.g., panic, discomfort, uncertainty) influence your response or actions?

_____

_____

_____

What could you have done differently to handle the situation more effectively?

_____

_____

_____

_____

How might your leadership change if you became more comfortable with not having all the answers, but focusing on helping others find their own?

_____

_____

_____

_____

GET TO KNOW YOUR PEOPLE

You can't be a good leader if you don't know your people.
— Colin Powell

People are the lifeblood of any organization. They are its most valuable asset, most important priority, and reason for being. Unlike other assets, however, every human being is unique. They come with different needs, priorities, skills, and quirks. As a leader, recognizing these differences and embracing them is crucial to building an engaged and motivated team. Providing individuals with the specific tools, resources, and support they need will not only help them to be successful but will also help the organization be successful. When leaders take the time to understand what drives their team members, they create an environment where people feel valued and empowered. The only way to do that is to get to know them. Understanding their strengths, challenges, and aspirations allows leaders to align individual and organizational goals for long-term success.

The exercises in Get to Know Your People are designed to help you build relationships with those around you and prioritize these relationships in expanding and strengthening your leadership.

24. The Power of the Follower

Followers are more important to leaders than leaders are to followers.
— BARBARA KELLERMAN

Leadership and followership, to me, are not that different. As I've said many times, we are all leaders, and in essence, we are all followers. For us individually, as well as for our collective teams and organizations, to be successful, we need to pay attention, cultivate our skills, and constantly develop ourselves to become our best selves. In some situations, we need to step forward, and at other times, we need to step back; it all depends on who we are working with and who is best to take the lead in that particular moment and with those particular people.

Exercise 24: Practice Following

Describe a recent project where you allowed someone else to take the lead. What was your role in the situation?

_____

_____

_____

_____

Why did you choose to step back and allow this person to lead? What made this the best decision for the situation?

_____

_____

_____

_____

How did your decision to step back contribute to the overall success of the team and the project?

_____

_____

_____

_____

Consider a project you're working on. Are there tasks you could delegate to someone else on your team? Identify a few areas where they could take the lead.

_____

_____

_____

_____

CREATE AN ACTION ITEM — GO TO PAGE 87

25. Building Trust

> *Earn trust, earn trust, earn trust. Then you can worry about the rest.*
> — SETH GODIN

There is absolutely nothing more important you can do as a leader than build trust with those around you. Trust is what brings teams together and keeps them together. It's what motivates team members to work hard and helps people to find satisfaction and security in their jobs. One of the primary ways we cultivate trust with our team is by listening to them, acknowledging their ideas, and creating an environment where they feel comfortable sharing their opinions.

Exercise 25: Building Trust Through Action

Think of a time when your team demonstrated trust in you. What did you do to earn their trust, and how did it impact the team's performance?

_____

_____

_____

_____

Consider what former Major League Baseball manager, Davey Johnson, said to me when I interviewed him for *Lead Me Out to the Ballgame.*

I don't care how long you've been in this game or what kind of success you've had in this game; every day, you have to gain their trust, and every day, you have to gain their respect.

What are some specific actions you can take as a leader to earn the trust of your team? List a few key actions you can implement.

1. _____

2. _____

3. _____

26. The "Platinum Rule"

> *We all grow up learning about the simplicity and power of the Golden Rule: Do unto others as you would want done to you. It's a splendid concept except for one thing: Everyone is different, and the truth is that in many cases what you'd want done to you is different from what your partner, employee, customer, investor, wife, or child would want done to him or her...The Golden Rule, as great as it is, has limitations, since all people and all situations are different. When you follow the Platinum Rule, however, you can be sure you're actually doing what the other person wants done and assure yourself of a better outcome.*
> — DAVE KERPEN

Everyone talks about the Golden Rule, which is, "treat everyone the way you want to be treated," and some talk about the Platinum Rule, described by author Dave Kerpen as treating everyone the way *they* want to be treated. In *Leadership in 5G,* we take this a step further and discuss an even more powerful, and to me, more important approach: We should treat others the way they *need* to be treated.

For many reasons, this is something we don't often consider. When we are pressed for time, limited with resources, or focused on our own style, we may incorrectly believe that what we would prefer in a certain situation is the same as what others do as well.

Exercise 26:

Think of a project you are currently or were recently working on with other members of your team. What are some of the ways that their work style differs from yours?

_____

_____

_____

_____

How did (or could) you set them up for success by adapting the way you work with them, assign them tasks, etc.?

_____

_____

_____

_____

Share one way you can strategically learn more about the styles of your team members. Head to the back of the book and create an Action Item.

_____

_____

_____

_____

27. Making Yourself Available – How Can I Help?

> *Trust is earned in the smallest of moments. It is earned not through heroic deeds, or even highly visible actions, but through paying attention, listening, and gestures of genuine care and connection.*
> — BRENÉ BROWN

Making ourselves available as a resource is one of the best ways to *lead by example*. By showing our team that we are there for them, we are providing support and also modeling behaviors that we want them to utilize in their own leadership journey. As much as our team may 'know' that we are available as a resource, reminding them of this on a continual basis is quite important.

Exercise 27: How Can I Help?

Name three people to whom you could ask the question, "How can I help?"

1. _____

2. _____

3. _____

What are some general reactions you anticipate from your team members when you ask the question?

_____

_____

_____

Action Step: Head to the back of the book and identify an action step (or two) from this exercise.

28. When You Ask for Feedback – Listen

> *The most basic of all human needs is the need to understand and be understood. The best way to understand people is to listen to them.*
> — RALPH NICHOL

We often have feedback mechanisms built into our organizations, but in a world of automation, sometimes these can become *too* automated. You might have surveys that go out to staff periodically, but what does the follow-up look like? Are staff actually feeling heard? If you ask for feedback, it's important to acknowledge it and to consider how it can possibly be utilized. We need to find frequent opportunities to garner feedback from those around us and provide feedback to those around us, formally and informally.

Put yourself in the shoes of someone that reports to you. If they had feedback, how do you think they would go about delivering it to you? Did you think they would come to you and share it openly? I encourage you to think about how often that's actually happened. If it hasn't, it's not necessarily a signal that your team doesn't have something to say, but rather, it could be a signal that:

- They don't know who to talk to
- They are concerned their feedback will be interpreted the wrong way
- Proactive communication is not their strength

…or any other number of obstacles.

Exercise 28: Improving the Cycle of Feedback

Choose three people on your team whose feedback is important to the team's success. (Note: You're starting with three, but everyone's feedback is important!) Make a plan to meet with each of them individually and ask them a couple questions, such as the following:

1. What are one or two areas where you feel the leadership team could gain greater clarity?
2. How could we improve our communication processes?
3. What do you wish everyone on the team understood better?

During these conversations, *focus on listening*; don't defend or counter what's being said. This is a time for you to simply receive the information and begin to process and consider it. Remember, the quality of your listening will contribute to the quality of the trust others have in you.

After these meetings, write what you learned from the process. Did anything surprise you?

_____

_____

_____

_____

What is one way you could improve the feedback gathering process for the whole organization?

_____

_____

_____

_____

CREATE AN ACTION ITEM — GO TO PAGE 87

29. Prioritize One-on-One's

> *The key to a good one-on-one meeting is the understanding that it is the employee's meeting rather than the manager's meeting.*
> — BEN HOROWITZ

One-on-one meetings are one of the most important meetings your organization will have, and they're also one of the easiest to neglect. These meetings should be structured so that both parties are clear as to their purpose, goals, and objectives, and you, no matter if you're the supervisor or report, should always enter the meeting with a bulleted list of items you wish to discuss. These items are not exhaustive, the meeting may veer off course, but at the minimum, these are the items you commit to addressing during the meeting.

Things to consider in creating your bulleted list before the one-on-one:

- What insights do I need that can't be conveyed in an email?
- What specific support or input do I and my team need from this person?
- How can I position myself as a stronger resource for them and the team?
- What are the key action items for both of us to take after the meeting?

Exercise 29: Make One-on-Ones Consistent

Look at your calendar. Do you have one-on-ones with each of your team members scheduled? The larger your team, the less frequently these meetings will be held, but no matter the size, meetings should be scheduled with your direct reports so that they know there is a formal opportunity to share information, discuss challenges, and look to you for opportunities to serve as a resource.

Using the questions above as a starting point, create some questions or prompts that are specific to you and your team that you can use to begin conversations during your one-on-ones.

1. _____
2. _____
3. _____
4. _____
5. _____

30. Create Memories that Matter

> *Good leaders build products. Great leaders build cultures. Good leaders deliver results.*
> *Great leaders develop people. Good leaders have vision. Great leaders have values.*
> *Good leaders are role models at work. Great leaders are role models in life.*
> — ADAM GRANT

A student of mine was having lunch in the cafeteria of the large insurance company where she worked when someone in a very expensive suit sat down and asked if he could dine with her. The person, she realized after recognizing him from his picture on the wall, was one of the executive vice presidents of the company. That interaction meant a lot to my student, as during their lunch, she was able to communicate her love for the company as well as some of the issues she was concerned about. During their lunch, the vice president told her he liked to chat informally with his team whenever he had a chance. This was something that she never forgot, and has used in her own leadership since. It doesn't take much to have an impact; a little bit of connection can go a long way.

Exercise 30:

Think of a time when a leader made you feel special and valued in the workplace. How did this interaction change the way you work?

How did this interaction change the way you approach your work or interact with others in the workplace?

_____

_____

_____

_____

As a leader, how can you create similar moments of connection with your team? What specific actions can you take to make them feel valued and heard?

_____

_____

_____

_____

GIVE THEM WHAT THEY NEED

To handle yourself, use your head; to handle others, use your heart.
— Eleanor Roosevelt

It's not enough to just get to know your people; you also need to meet their needs. Some of those needs are expressed, and some might not be, like mentorship, training, and feedback. Some needs are general and apply to all people, such as respect, while others are more specific to those you are working with. Giving your people what they need means paying attention to all of these things and making meeting needs your priority. By doing so, you create a culture of support and trust, where team members feel valued and motivated. When leaders focus on fulfilling their people's needs, they foster an environment that encourages growth, collaboration, and long-term success.

The exercises in Give Them What They Need are designed to help you identify what your people need and encourage them to give their best to the organization.

31. A New Generation of Needs

We're so much more alike than we are different. At the core of it all, we're all feeling the same feelings of fear and sadness and loneliness and happiness and love.
— Olivia Rodrigo

Step back and think about your team. What do they really want? What do they really need? What matters most to them? You might think bonuses, promotions, and pay raises are what people always want, but the latest studies are showing that those things aren't the greatest motivators, particularly for Gen Z. People today are looking for flexibility, purpose-filled work, recognition, and a positive organizational culture. Remember, leadership isn't about us; it's about 'them'.

Exercise 31: How Much Do I Really Know You?

Your job as a leader isn't just to manage; it's to inspire, support, and create an environment where people thrive. Let's see how well you understand your team.

What motivates your team beyond salary and promotions? Identify at least three non-financial factors that drive engagement and satisfaction in your team.

1. _____
2. _____
3. _____
4. _____
5. _____

In what ways do your leadership approach, workplace culture, or company practices align with or challenge what your team values most?

_____
_____
_____
_____

What's one small but meaningful change you can make right away to better align your leadership with what your team truly needs?

___

___

___

___

Bonus: Schedule a team meeting and have a round table discussion on this topic.

1. Set the scene: Make sure everyone knows that the tone and temper of this conversation should be curiosity and understanding. Have each of the people you invite consider some of the ways they define leadership, consider their motivators, and think about the ways the organization is meeting and not meeting their expectations.
2. Make a list on a whiteboard or projector:

    a. What are the positive aspects of each generation?
    b. What does each generation wish the other one(s) understood better?
    c. What are some potential blind spots of each generation?
    d. What are some things all the generations share?

3. Host a discussion: Ask the members of each generation to confirm or dispute the characteristics on the list in the spirit of curiosity.
4. Take action: Come up with at least one action item that the team can put into motion immediately after leaving the meeting.

32. Psychological Safety and Building Confidence

> *Psychological safety does not mean that you feel comfortable all the time. Psychological safety means you feel comfortable talking about what makes you uncomfortable.*
> — Esther Derby

Psychological safety is a term coined by Harvard professor Amy Edmonson and is a concept that is quite important in today's workplace. The term is used to describe an environment where people feel safe to express their opinions and safe to fail without fear of retribution.

Exercise 32: "The Anxiety Party"

In a group setting, have each team member spend 10 minutes writing down their biggest anxieties at work. It could be project-related (our deadlines on these reports are too close together), anything that impacts the day-to-day (I lose valuable time because we have no coffee on this floor), or personal (I've had to miss work because of my child's health issues, and I worry the team doesn't think I'm pulling my weight).

Go around the room and take turns sharing the anxieties. To make this activity even more psychologically safe, you could consider having these anxieties put in a box or submitted anonymously. Notice any repeated topics that come up.

The point of this exercise is to give the team a safe space to share their frustrations without fear of retribution. It also gives you a chance to identify some of the team's pain points and immediately come up with action items together to solve the issues.

Write three things that you learned about your team and three Action Items that you can take from what you learned.

1. _____

2. _____

3. _____

Action Items:

1. _____

2. _____

3. _____

33. Help Others See the Mission and Vision

If your actions inspire others to dream more, learn more, do more, and become more, you are a leader.
— John Quincy Adams

For people to commit to a change, it's important that they understand how the change is going to impact them specifically. A part of helping others see their part in the mission is their answer to the question WIIFM: What's in it for me? Getting someone to "buy in" to a change, and to make your goals their goals, is a skill. Teachers use it, parents use it, coaches use it, and great leaders in every industry use it with great results. If we want our people to join us and work with us toward a goal, they need to understand how the goal aligns with their own individual needs and vision.

Exercise 33: Inspiring Buy-In Through Personal Impact

Identify a specific initiative or change that you will introduce to your team.

_____
_____
_____
_____

How will this change benefit the group as a whole?

_____
_____
_____
_____

What personal benefit will each individual gain from this change?

_____

_____

_____

_____

How can you communicate this change in a way that each individual understands the specific benefits they will reap?

_____

_____

_____

_____

CREATE AN ACTION ITEM — GO TO PAGE 87

34. Trust and Respect

> As we look ahead into the next century, leaders will be those who empower others.
> — BILL GATES

I believe that when someone is promoted to a higher position, they should be given your respect, as I assume they were promoted for good reason! That said, they won't maintain that trust and respect just because of the position; they need to continue to earn it each day. I encourage my clients to have an open mind and give someone a chance when they are promoted, but I also watch to see whether they are living up to their responsibilities and acting as leaders in their new roles.

Exercise 34: Promotion Transitions

Describe the steps you take to help a new manager transition into their new role, especially if they were previously a peer.

_____
_____
_____
_____

What signs do you look for to determine if they are successfully fulfilling their role, and would you address concerns?

_____
_____
_____
_____

What strategies do you use to check in with your team and foster a smooth transition during leadership changes?

_____
_____
_____
_____

35. The Right Seat on the Bus

Great vision without great people is irrelevant.
— Jim Collins

Jim Collins had a great metaphor in his book *Good to Great*: You've got to get the right people on the bus and get them in the right seats. Giving people work that fits their skill sets is a critical part of giving them what they need. Assessing the status of your "bus" should be a regular activity. Take time to do these reflective exercises at least twice a year, and have your team do this as well.

Exercise 35: The Wheels on the Bus

Wrong seat: Identify one team member who consistently struggles and seems like they may not be matched for their task.

_____

Is there a different seat on the bus for them? If they are a good fit for the organization (or even the team), is there a more fitting role for them?

_____

Next seat: Identify one team member who consistently excels (and doesn't seem to be pressuring themselves to do so!):

_____

Is it time to promote them or adjust their tasks to keep them challenged and interested? What specifically could you do to help them remain engaged?

_____

_____

_____

New seat: Identify one hole on your team, a task or role that is not being addressed.

_____

_____

_____

Is there an opportunity to hire or promote someone to fill the team's goals?

_____

_____

_____

_____

CREATE AN ACTION ITEM → GO TO PAGE 87

Go further:

Identify 3 team members and inventory their strengths and any tasks they consistently struggle with. Are their roles aligned with their areas of expertise? What is one way you could adjust a responsibility, assign a task to a better-suited teammate, or provide coaching to help them thrive?

TEAM MEMBER	STRENGTHS	TASKS THEY STRUGGLE WITH	SUGGESTED ADJUSTMENTS

Ask those three team members what aspect of their role excites them most and what they'd prefer to spend less time on. Use their feedback to inform your next steps.

What I learned:

_____

_____

_____

_____

CREATE AN ACTION ITEM — GO TO PAGE 87

36. Training

> *Leaders are made, they are not born. They are made by hard effort, which is the price which all of us must pay to achieve any goal that is worthwhile.*
> — Vince Lombardi

After you've established that you have the right people in the right positions, they still need the training and resources to get the job done. Training should be an ongoing process that begins with a formal onboarding and never ends. Leaders, which we all are, have a focus on continuous improvement for themselves and those around them.

Exercise 36: Training Day

Do a survey of your team members. What training are they interested in? Encourage them to do some research on what might be useful for their current role as well as one they are striving to achieve. Ask them to identify a workshop, online training, or conference that would help them in their job or help the department or organization in general. If cost is a factor, work with your team member to find alternatives once a focus is determined.

Assign someone on your team to compile this list with other opportunities that you have identified.

Remember, for an organization to succeed, its people need to perform at a high level on both the soft and the 'hard' skills.

Before we ask our team, we should consider ourselves. What are some specific training opportunities that you feel would benefit you and/or your team?

1. _____

2. _____

3. _____

CREATE AN ACTION ITEM — GO TO PAGE 87

37. Mentorship

> *The delicate balance of mentoring someone is not creating them in your own image, but giving them the opportunity to create themselves.*
> — STEVEN SPIELBERG

Many mentoring programs fail because there isn't enough intentionality in the process. The ones that I have seen and created for organizations incorporate a *formal* structure in an *informal* way. The exercise below, also included in the book, gives a blueprint for kicking off a mentoring program at your company.

Exercise 37: Mentorship That Actually Works

Organize a networking event for your organization. Consider an event that fits the culture of your organization or team. Look at your calendar and identify a time when it can be held.

_____

_____

_____

_____

Task your employees with the goal of meeting three new people during the event. Write three conversation starters related to the workplace that attendees can use to spark discussion.

1. _____

2. _____

3. _____

CREATE AN ACTION ITEM — GO TO PAGE 87

38. Feedback

Criticism, like rain, should be gentle enough to nourish a man's growth without destroying his roots.
— Frank A. Clark

We never want our team to wonder whether they're doing a good job with their projects or assignments. If they have doubts and hesitations, they probably aren't putting their full potential or effort into their work. We're more motivated to perform when we're confident in our ability, which is why training and feedback are so important. Whether good or bad, there is always room for improvement, and it's our job to provide the tools and guidance to those we work with to continue their development.

Exercise 38: Providing Effective Feedback

Identify a team member or colleague you will provide feedback to in the near future.

_____

_____

_____

_____

Consider a specific behavior or performance area you want to address. What are some of your goals for the feedback? What benefits do you hope to achieve?

_____

_____

_____

_____

Write out three specific points you want to express, including both positive and negative aspects. Remember, whether the feedback is positive or negative, it should always have a developmental tone.

1. _____

2. _____

3. _____

39. Helping Others Build the Life They Want

> *Leadership is service, not position.*
> — Tim Fargo

Chances are, your team, much like you, is striving to build a life, not just a career. As people seek a greater work/life balance and lean into purpose-driven jobs, their definition of success has evolved from what it might have been a few decades ago. Your role as a leader is not to guide people into the life you think they should lead, but to help them learn, grow, and express themselves in ways that enable them to become their best selves.

Understanding what your team values requires curiosity. You need to get to know them, their lives, and what motivates them. Today's workers seek a more fulfilling work/life balance, and it's essential that we all contribute to creating a culture where this balance is cultivated.

Exercise 39: The Strategic Insight Team

Create and distribute a survey to your team, asking what's most important to them in the workplace and in their jobs (a quick online search can give you plenty of sample questions, but try to personalize it to your department and organization). Next, form a team of representatives from different departments (finance, IT, HR, etc.) to come together and review the survey results. Have them discuss feasible changes and propose an actionable plan that demonstrates your commitment to helping employees build the life they want.

Finally, identify individuals who would be a good fit for your Insight Team and craft an email inviting them to participate in this initiative. Your goal is to create a proposal that shows your dedication to supporting your team's needs and aspirations.

What are the top three things your team values most in the workplace?

1. _____

2. _____

3. _____

What questions would you include in the survey to gain insights into their needs? Write five personalized questions you would ask to help understand what drives your team members.

1. _____

2. _____

3. _____

4. _____

5. _____

Draft a brief message that explains the project's goals and why you're seeking their participation.

_____

_____

_____

_____

Based on the insights you gather, what are some actionable steps you could take to support your team's work/life balance and personal growth?

_____

_____

_____

_____

40. Rejuvenation

Almost everything will work again if you unplug it for a few minutes, including you.
— ANNE LAMOTT.

Sharing your passion and values is like sharing energy. When you bring others into what excites you and show them how it can benefit them too, you create momentum. When people commit with you toward a shared goal, those wins feel even bigger. These wins don't just push you forward; they recharge you. That's real rejuvenation.

This cycle of shared passion and success fuels you as a leader, too. In the daily grind, it's easy to forget that true rejuvenation isn't just about taking time off; it comes from reconnecting with what truly matters. By aligning your passions with the people you lead, you not only help them succeed but also refresh yourself.

Exercise 40:

Recall a time you felt truly energized at work. What were you doing? Who was involved? How did sharing your passion impact the experience?

_____

_____

_____

_____

Think of a current goal. How can you engage others in it? List 2-3 ways to bring them in and build momentum together.

The goal: _____

How can you engage others in it?

_____

_____

_____

_____

What can you do to help your team find meaning in their work and stay motivated? List three actions you can take to inspire and recharge them.

1. _____

2. _____

3. _____

Bonus Challenge: Plan a Rejuvenation Event

A thriving team is one that feels supported and valued. Beyond sharing our passions toward our work, consider implementing special initiatives to help your team recharge. Whether it's a small gesture like a catered meal or a larger event like a mindfulness retreat, investing in your team's well-being leads to stronger performance and satisfaction.

Identify three events/initiatives that can help your team rejuvenate:

1. _____

2. _____

3. _____

CREATE AN ACTION ITEM — GO TO PAGE 87

41. Leading in Uncertain Times

Courage is not the absence of fear. It is going forward with the face of fear.
— ABRAHAM LINCOLN

Leading is a challenge in normal times, let alone during times of uncertainty. Whether the uncertainty is external, coming from your industry or political/social climate, or internal from within your organization itself, when we feel our stress or our security threatened, it can be easy to turn inward to protect ourselves. As a leader, during these times is when our team needs us the most.

There will be times you need to lead your team through uncertainty, conflict, and stress. Layoffs, management or administration changes, a pandemic, or changes in the political landscape can lead our team to concern and worry about their jobs, the organization, or even their industry. In these circumstances, we need to help our people, engage them, and inspire them in a way that's going to keep them motivated to perform.

Exercise 41:

Consider what could be causing uncertainty for your people right now. What are those things that could be adding stress to their day to day lives? Be specific, and in the space below, write down the names of individuals and/or teams that are feeling pressure of some kind.

_____

_____

_____

_____

What are some tangible and specific ways you could provide support to your team right now? Remember, in addition to the individual stress each team member may be feeling, they also have individual ways to deal with the stress. Think of each person as an individual and consider the best ways and tools to use in assisting them.

_____

_____

_____

_____

GET OUT OF THE WAY!

Leaders don't create followers, they create more leaders
— Tom Peters

The real win in leadership is developing other leaders. But that only happens when you loosen the reins and give people room to learn, even if that means they'll make some mistakes along the way. You brought them in for a reason, so trust them. Let them step up, take ownership, and show you what they can do. As they gain experience and confidence, they will grow into roles that will ultimately strengthen the entire organization. Supporting their growth means giving them the opportunity to take initiative and challenge themselves. In the process, you'll not only build a stronger team but also foster a culture of empowerment and accountability.

The exercises in Get Out of the Way are designed to help you inspire leadership in others and to recognize when it is your turn to step back and follow their lead.

42. A Well-Oiled Machine

Don't tell people how to do things, tell them what to do and let them surprise you with their results.
— GEORGE S. PATTON

A team that functions like a well-oiled machine is one where everyone has clarity on what is and isn't their responsibility. The team works well together, with all necessary tasks for a job well done assigned to someone. Each member is trustworthy, and there is a sense of autonomy, allowing team members to make basic decisions without the need for constant oversight. This clarity, trust, and autonomy create a cohesive and efficient team dynamic, where everyone is empowered to contribute their best work.

Exercise 42: Roadblocks

List three things that get in the way of your team running like a well-oiled machine.

1. _____

2. _____

3. _____

To operate as a well-oiled machine, team members need to feel like they *own* the process and are empowered to move forward without oversight. To do this, we need to step back and allow them to perform.

What are three tasks you currently handle that you could delegate to team members to increase their sense of ownership?

1. _____

2. _____

3. _____

43. Decision-Making

A problem clearly stated is a problem half solved.
— DOROTHEA BRANDE

In many situations, people are expected to follow us simply because of the structure of the job. Real leadership, as we've explored, isn't about obligation; it's about creating an environment where people *want* to follow. When we give our team the chance to make real decisions and have a say in the process, we're not just leading, we're empowering, and that's what builds true buy-in and commitment to our goals.

Exercise 43: Extending Decision-Making

Think about an upcoming project or initiative (big or small) where you could trust your team to take the lead. Do you have the right people? Are the right people in the right roles? Do you need to provide your team with further training prior to beginning the project?

What is the project, and what specific steps can you take to prepare them to lead it to success?

_____

_____

_____

_____

List three ways you can serve as a resource to the team during the project (as well as the planning stages) while still allowing them to take the lead.

1. _____

2. _____

3. _____

44. Situational Leadership

Knowledge is knowing that a tomato is a fruit; wisdom is not putting it in a fruit salad.
— MILES KINGTON

All the strength in the world is useless when you're trying to peel a boiled egg. Some situations require courage, others gentleness. You don't just want to be a strong and knowledgeable leader; you want to be a wise one, too. Situational leadership is wise leadership.

Exercise 44: Back and Forward

Reflect on a recent time when you led "too much" and a recent time when you led "too little." How could you have handled each scenario differently?

A time I led "too much"

_____

_____

_____

_____

The impact I had on the situation

_____

_____

_____

_____

A time I led "too little"

_____

_____

_____

_____

The impact I had on the situation

_____

_____

_____

_____

Identify best practices you can extract from these situations.

_____

_____

_____

_____

CREATE AN ACTION ITEM — GO TO PAGE 87

45. Leading People Toward the "Win"

> *To build a strong team, you must see someone else's strength as a complement to your weakness and not a threat to your position or authority.*
> — CHRISTINE CAINE

Depending on your interests and experience, you may have different visuals come to mind when I say the word "winning." Regardless of whether your passion is for athletics or music, gaming or cooking, we all know what it feels like to know that we've succeeded. A win is a win, and it feels good to win!

Part of leading people toward the win is inviting them into the process of making plays. The following exercise can be pivotal in your team's ownership of their collective future.

Exercise 45: Stop, Start, Continue

At your next team meeting, get a whiteboard or easel and draw three columns labeled stop, start, and continue. Give a pad of sticky notes to each member of the team and have them write down the things they believe the team should start doing, stop doing, and continue doing. (This can also be done on a virtual whiteboard via Zoom.) At the end of the exercise, have team members vote on which items they think should be prioritized in each column. Most importantly, ensure that the meeting ends with action items for each member of the team. This exercise has the potential to engender great trust among the team, but only if leadership is willing to follow through.

For now, consider this for yourself: What are some things your team should stop, start, and continue to perform at their best?

_____

_____

_____

_____

What is something your team should *stop* doing that is hindering progress or efficiency?

_____

_____

_____

_____

What is something your team should *start* doing to improve collaboration, productivity, or morale?

_____

_____

_____

_____

What is something your team should *continue* doing that is working well and should be maintained or expanded?

___

___

___

___

46. A Continual Focus on the "Next Thing"

> *I don't care how much power, brilliance or energy you have, if you don't harness it and focus it on a specific target, and hold it there, you're never going to accomplish as much as your ability warrants.*
> — Zig Ziglar

To succeed, you need clarity on your goal and a clear plan to achieve it. Success isn't just about individual accomplishments; it's about lifting up the entire team. The key is to break down your goal into actionable steps, ensuring everyone is aligned and working together toward the same vision. With a solid action plan in place, you can focus on winning as a team, not just as individuals.

Exercise 46: Is Everyone On the Same Page?

To achieve success, it's important to break your goal down into clear, actionable steps. This process ensures everyone understands their role and how they contribute to the team's overall success. By defining the goal, outlining the necessary actions, and assigning responsibilities, you create a roadmap that helps the team stay on track and focused on what truly matters. Now, let's map out the path to success.

What is the specific goal you want your team to achieve? Be as clear and measurable as possible. Write down the goal and make sure it aligns with the larger vision of your team or organization.

_____

_____

_____

_____

What are the key steps your team needs to take to achieve this goal? List out the major actions and milestones that will guide your team toward success. Include any resources or support needed for each step.

KEY STEP	ACTION/MILESTONE	RESOURCES/SUPPORT NEEDED

Who is responsible for each step, and when should it be completed? Ensure that each action step is assigned to a team member and that realistic deadlines are set. How will you keep track of progress and hold each other accountable?

STEP/ACTION	RESPONSIBLE TEAM MEMBER	DEADLINE	PROGRESS TRACKING	ACCOUNTABILITY METHOD

Next steps:

_____

_____

_____

_____

47. The Link Between Winning and Purpose

> *When you have balance in your life, work becomes an entirely different experience. There is a passion that moves you to a whole new level of fulfillment and gratitude, and that's when you can do your best, for yourself and for others.*
> — CARA DELEVINGNE

Crushing a performance goal or landing a big deal is definitely a win, and it feels great. Hitting your goals is crucial to keeping a company running, but anyone who's been around for a while knows that while financial and numerical success is exciting, it's not the ultimate win we're really after. Just like we strive for that ideal work/life balance for ourselves, we should be helping our team chase that same goal, too.

Exercise 47: Striking a Balance

What does work/life balance mean to you? How do you define it, and how does it impact your work and well-being?

_____

_____

_____

_____

Identify three changes you can make in your daily routine to move closer to that ideal balance.

1. _____

2. _____

3. _____

How can you create a supportive environment for your team to pursue their own balance while still hitting their goals?

_____

_____

_____

_____

48. Learning From Mistakes

> *Mistakes are the portals of discovery.*
> — James Joyce

Mistakes happen all the time. We make them. Our people make them. Everyone makes them. The key to leadership is understanding what our mistakes are, learning from them, and making sure that we use those mistakes as a way to help others avoid the same ones. Consider each mistake you make as a teaching tool, and your team will benefit each day.

Exercise 48: We Live and Learn

Describe a recent mistake you've made. What did you learn from the experience?

_____
_____
_____
_____

How can this mistake be used to help your team avoid similar issues?

_____
_____
_____
_____

Create a plan to share this mistake with your team as a valuable learning opportunity.

___

___

___

___

49. When We Are Proactive, We Don't Need to Be Reactive

> *The best executive is the one who has sense enough to pick good people to do what he wants done, and self-restraint enough to keep from meddling with them while they do it.*
> — THEODORE ROOSEVELT

It's easiest to "get out of the way" when you've done the right work at the beginning. You've gotten to know yourself and your team, you've communicated well, and you've properly equipped those around you to do the work they need to do. When these things are in place and a crisis comes up, both you and your team should know how to handle it. Our goal should always be to act as proactively as possible so that we don't need to react in a haste.

Exercise 50: Laying the Foundation for Proactive Leadership

Proactive leadership is about laying a strong foundation early on so that when challenges arise, you and your team are already prepared to handle them effectively. By investing time upfront in understanding your team, setting clear expectations, and empowering others, you reduce the need for reactive decision-making in moments of crisis. This exercise will help you evaluate your preparedness and take proactive steps to strengthen your leadership.

Consider how clearly you've set expectations for your team and empowered them to take ownership of their roles. Write down specific steps you can take to improve their autonomy and confidence in handling tasks independently.

1. _____

2. _____

3. _____

Assess your understanding of your team's strengths and weaknesses. How can you gain a deeper awareness of their capabilities and areas for growth?

1. _____

2. _____

3. _____

What specific actions can you take to strengthen your team's ability to solve problems independently?

1. _____

2. _____

3. _____

50. Leaving a Legacy

*People will forget what you said, people will forget what you did,
but people will never forget how you made them feel.*
— Maya Angelou

Legacy is the trail we leave behind; the impact of our words and actions stays with people long after we've moved on. What we do and how we do it shapes the people we lead, the teams we build, and the culture we create. Remember, it's not just about the things we accomplish, but how we make others feel, challenge them to grow, and empower them to do their best. Every interaction leaves a mark, and we should use our leadership to make it one that lifts people up.

Exercise 49: A Life Worth Living

How would you like to be remembered? Define the legacy you hope to leave behind.

_____

_____

_____

_____

Identify three specific ways you can do *more* to create the legacy you desire:

1. _____

2. _____

3. _____

Congratulations on Your Upgrade to 5G!

You've read the book, considered the implications and application of the 5Gs of leadership, and now, through the Companion Workbook, you've explored how they can be applied and included in your leadership toolkit.

As you know, *Leadership in 5G: Practical Strategies for Individual, Team, and Organizational Success* doesn't end after the 5th G; there's a bonus one, which is the key to an even greater connection. We need to **Get to Work***!*

I trust that the 50 exercises in this workbook have been a valuable resource, but just like in *Leadership in 5G*, the real work is only just beginning. I hope you've already started filling in your Action Items on the following pages, but if not, or if new ideas have come to you, I encourage you to take a moment to write them down now. Throughout this workbook, you've been prompted to create action steps based on each exercise. If you haven't completed them yet, I urge you to go back through the workbook and solidify your plans. What you've accomplished here is a foundation—now it's time for execution. Refine your action items, set your start (and completion) dates, and **Get to Work!**

If you need additional support with your leadership upgrade, whether individually or as a team, let's discuss how I can assist you through coaching, training programs, or a keynote address at your organization. You can reach me at howard@theleadershipdoc.com.

Congrats again on your upgrade, and keep leading!

Howard C. Fero, PhD
The Leadership Doc
March 2025

ACTION ITEMS

MY UPGRADE TO 5G!

As you work through this Companion Workbook, use this area to record Action Items based on the exercises. Whenever possible, include a start date and projected end date to help guide your progress.

	ACTIVITY/TASK	START DATE	END DATE	COMPLETE
1				☐
2				☐
3				☐
4				☐
5				☐
6				☐

ACTIVITY/TASK	START DATE	END DATE	COMPLETE
7			☐
8			☐
9			☐
10			☐
11			☐
12			☐
13			☐
14			☐
15			☐

	ACTIVITY/TASK	START DATE	END DATE	COMPLETE
16				☐
17				☐
18				☐
19				☐
20				☐
21				☐
22				☐
23				☐
24				☐

ACTIVITY/TASK	START DATE	END DATE	COMPLETE
25			☐
26			☐
27			☐
28			☐
29			☐
30			☐
31			☐
32			☐
33			☐

ACTIVITY/TASK	START DATE	END DATE	COMPLETE
34			☐
35			☐
36			☐
37			☐
38			☐
39			☐
40			☐
41			☐
42			☐

ACTIVITY/TASK	START DATE	END DATE	COMPLETE
43			☐
44			☐
45			☐
46			☐
47			☐
48			☐
49			☐
50			☐

www.ingramcontent.com/pod-product-compliance
Lightning Source LLC
Chambersburg PA
CBHW060426010526
44118CB00017B/2376